TWO BACKPACKS

TWO BACKPACKS

Learning Their Story and Building Relationships with a Trauma Informed Perspective

ADOLPH BROWN

CreateSpace 4900 LaCross Road
North Charleston, SC 29406 USA

CreateSpace books may be ordered through booksellers or by contacting:
CreateSpace
4900 LaCross Road North Charleston, SC 29406
USA
Because of the dynamic nature of the Internet, any Web addresses or links contained in this book may have changed since publication and may no longer be valid. The views expressed in this work are solely those of the author and do not necessarily reflect the views of the publisher, and the publisher hereby disclaims any responsibility for them.

ISBN 13: 9781546646426

ISBN 10: 1546646426

Printed in the United States of America

TABLE OF CONTENTS

FOREWORD

As a Family Physician, I often see people with stress related illnesses that stem from problems in the home, school, or work place. Medicines can help with, but not solve, these problems. Helping individuals with these problems requires more than just looking at their physical health. Psychologic health and "social health" are just as important.

Having known and worked with Dr. Adolph Brown for many years, he never ceases to amaze me with his depth of knowledge and understanding of the human condition. As a university professor, clinical psychologist, and corporate consultant he has researched and gained extensive experience in helping individuals, families, schools, and businesses with problems extending across the psychological and relationship spectrum.

In "Two Backpacks" Dr. Brown tackles the difficult subject of dealing with individuals with a difficult past who exhibit difficult behaviors.

No matter what you do for a living, one of the most challenging aspects of work is dealing with others. Those who are tasked with teaching, supervising, or managing others, are often left with the difficult task of understanding, and motivating those for whom they are in charge. Those being taught or managed are often faced with uneven management styles and unclear expectations.

This is especially true in the in the field of education. Classroom teachers have the difficult task of teaching a group of students with varying levels of interest, skills, and motivation. "Difficult children (students)" – those who won't or can't participate and cooperate - are particularly challenging. They often cause disruptions in the classroom and can make teaching and learning all but impossible.

Instead of being met with patience and understanding, these children are often met with dread and disdain. In order to help these children, we must first understand them. In this book, Dr. Brown gives a practical and easy to understand framework for dealing with the difficult behaviors exhibited by others, whether they be children in a classroom or executives in a board room.

For those of us who find ourselves in these difficult situations (and most of us will), the "Two Backpacks" approach gives the tools to both understand and cope with the difficult behaviors exhibited by others – and by ourselves!

This book will leave you educated, motivated, inspired, entertained and ready to make a difference in your family, community, and work place.

Gregory W. Pierce, M.D.
Author: *Building Health, Building Wellness*
— A Common Sense Approach to Health Enhancement
Carrollton, Virginia
2017

INTRODUCTION

I have been tremendously blessed to travel the world, yes the world, on a journey to spread love, light and insight everywhere I'm invited. This book was inspired by the countless in-person and written comments I have received from education and corporate leaders regarding how their people have not overcome the challenges of relating to people who are different from themselves. Many of these leaders have reached out to me in urgency as "relationship building" is the hallmark of their enterprise. In the "sensitive issues" portion of my project management consultation form, I have read many distressing comments about of how employees have missed the relational mark with regards to customer service, student & parent engagement, community outreach, community policing, hospitality management, physician "bedside manner" and restaurant hosting to name a few. Here are a few things overheard:

> **"What is wrong with that person?"**
> **"I would hate to be his/her parents!!"**

"Some people are just very difficult to work with."

"I can't help people I don't get."

"This student has so much stuff going on in his life, being in school is a waste of time."

Written comments have looked like this:

"Many of our staff are not accustomed to serving our demographics, as they do not have any points of reference for individuals unlike themselves."

"My middle-class teachers are having a rough time dealing with children and families from other socioeconomic classes."

"Our officers need immediate help recognizing their blind spots. Our goal is to help each of them utilize strict self-discipline in putting prejudices aside and looking deeper into everything we do."

"My team members are falling into the trap of only looking at the surface of people, things, and ideas without taking the time and effort to delve deeper."

It is important to recognize that we all have significant emotional burdens and complications. And all relationships have breaks and repairs. I have been quite successful helping individuals call on their empathy to maintain consistent and caring relationships.

This book is the first in a series and I find it paramount to devote it to our future, our children. The aforementioned statements present relational quandaries daily for adults and children alike. However, I believe as does Frederick Douglas that "It is easier to build strong children than to repair broken men." If only we knew each other's story, I think we would all be a gentler and kinder people. Relationship building starts with empathy. Students enter our schools daily burdened by the effects of trauma and loss. They have experienced many events that most adults with coping strategies and support systems still have difficulty handling. Many children have histories of early neglect, abuse and attachment separation from parents. The burden becomes significantly heavier if the child is experiencing ongoing and pervasive stress of exposure to community violence, domestic violence, grief and abandonment issues due to parental loss, and chronic poverty. The results of these experiences often leave our young feeling guarded, apprehensive, anxious, and frightened. This child can be a challenging student based on his or her feelings that the world is unsafe. I think there are numerous adults whose *modus operandi* fits this child. Examples of this are seen with some "supergun owners" or individuals who own an average of 17 guns each. Researchers at the Harvard Injury Control Center have found that the top reason people owned guns was for protection from other people, even though the rate of violent crime has dropped significantly the past two decades. Another example involves "preppers" or individuals who believe a catastrophic disaster or emergency is likely to occur in the future and make active preparations for it, typically by stockpiling food, ammunition and other supplies.

These individuals have an overactive fight-or-flight response and are constantly scanning the environment for dangerous cues. These are significant emotional burdens for all, and the truth of the matter is that we all have some degree of these types of burdens.

CHAPTER 1

SAVING ADEL

A del was a seven-year-old boy who would constantly get into fights in school and in his community, none of which he would start. However, Adel was small for his age and believed most of his peers to be violent and unpredictable. Disagreements often resulted in physical confrontations, like when Adel and Marcus Smith couldn't decide whose turn it was to use the swing set. Marcus picked up a brick cinderblock and struck Adel across his eye causing an injury that required multiple sutures. Adel's parents divorced when he was only two-years-old and he was left to grow up without a dad, in the inner-city projects, with his single-parent mother, his older brother and three sisters. He would often witness physical and gun violence in his community. Unconsciously, Adel refused to be a victim like the people he would often see lying in pools of blood or those individuals who would have to be carried to the entrance of his community to receive medical attention from ambulance and rescue personnel.

(Even first responders were concerned about their safety in Adel's community.)

Adel had many supports in place as his mother was an avid supporter of education and would often swiftly reprimand Adel for any school-related infractions. Adel's great aunt was his cornerstone as she was the matriarch in his family and lived nearby. His maternal grandfather was his hero.

Although Adel continued to excel in school and sports, his response to agitation did not wane. Of his most ardent supporters were his head start and public school elementary school teachers, Mrs. Katie Sneade – Head Start, Mrs. Caroll Venning-First Grade, Mrs. Mary Lee Hertzog-Second Grade, and Mrs. Susan Tolley-Third Grade. His elementary school principal, Mr. Ralph Mizelle, even cheered for Adel in the classroom and on the athletic fields. All of these supporters played a significant role in Adel's young life. They were crucial when, at eleven years old, Adel's brother and oldest sibling was murdered.

Adel's family was unable to curb his appetite for response to provocation, so his mother and aunt enrolled him into martial arts to help him control his emotions. Adel excelled in karate, and was even less temperamental in other settings. Some would argue that enrolling Adel in a combative sport would have reinforced his aggressive tendencies, however, it was Adel's feelings of vulnerability in an unsafe environment that triggered his maladaptive responses to perceived and real provocation. Today, researchers would say that Adel was persistently traumatized and his brain structure changed to adapt to his belief of the presence of constant threat. From a research perspective without caring adults, connection to an achievement-oriented activity and three high-performing elementary teachers in a row, Adel may not have grown up to be a fifth degree black belt in karate, a full tenured university professor, research scientist and award-winning academic dean, but most importantly a happily married husband and father.

Society cheers loudly for the "bad boy" turned good man, however there are Adels and Adellas everyday who do not make it out of their traumatized circumstances. They are often the "invisible high-risk" children, perceived "throw-away" children who people have given up on, or the hopeless and helpless children who no one knows how to help. I will share stories that will help you recognize the burdens that people secretly carry, as well as help you to nurture and grow the tree that lies within every seed. I am thankful for all of my supporters, encouragers and growers for not killing the seed before it had an opportunity to grow. Adel was the common mispronunciation of my name Adolph while growing in the projects. Thank you for saving me!

CHAPTER 2

LOSING MARY

Mary is a thirteen-year-old girl who comes to school exhausted and falls asleep in her classes. She is unable to concentrate and is often easily irritated and agitated. This year, Mary has been less able to control her temper outbursts, has accumulated many absences, is less engaged in school activities and is in jeopardy of repeating the grade. Mary is often sent to the school counselor and the assistant principal for verbal abuse of her teachers, and sometimes for causing destruction of property. Following numerous disciplinary referrals and interventions, Mary begins to share events of her home life. She shares that her mother is her only friend and she doesn't intentionally do anything to displease her. She says she does not know why she is so angry and upset most of the time. Mary lives with her father and her step-mother and has weekend visitation with her mother. Many of the adults in Mary's life assume that Mary is devastated by her parents' divorce five years prior.

Her assistant principal believes that Mary has become jealous regarding the amount of time her mother spends with her multiple boyfriends. The school counselor recognizes that Mary's behavior is grossly out of proportion to the triggers of being asked to wake up during class, frequent prompts to pay attention and verbal reprimands regarding missing homework assignments. Tearfully, Mary reveals a secret she has being carrying around for over five years. Her school counselor supported her retelling of her traumatic past. Mary was ashamed, guilty and blamed herself for what had been occurring. She didn't want to stop seeing her mother or get her mother into trouble. Mary had been a victim of repeated sexual molestation.

How did this abuse go unnoticed under the watchful and mandated reporter eyes of her teachers? Often we react to situations before reflecting on them. Should Mary have been allowed to sleep in class, as her bad dreams at night often would keep her awake? I share with educators who may be unaware of what to do in certain situations that a simple "How may I help you?" will suffice. Mary's behavior became so disrespectful and violent that some educators were despised with her presence. It was often overheard in the teacher's lounge about the many times she "went off" today. Diagnoses were also debated. However, the adults in her life rarely brainstormed ways to prevent her from becoming enraged, nor did they debate alternative explanations for her behavior.

Although teachers should be able to teach in safe and respectable environments, often we have to ensure that we are doing all we can to keep it that way. I have grown to believe that children need a way out of potentially volatile situations, and it is also fine for them to "win." As far as we know this may be the only time this student has ever come out on top. And yes, the rest of the classroom may be observing the exchanges, however every student is different just as children are within the same family. What works with one child may not work with another. I believe this is the crux of differentiated teaching strategies – differentiated relational strategies. We have to remember that we are human-beings working with developing human-beings.

"Two Backpacks" is simply an analogy used for the student who enters any classroom with the one backpack we see for supplies, and the one we do not see, "their story." The same is true for adults, be it two purses or two wallets. There are aspects of our lives that drive our behavior that are unbeknownst to most, even our dearest and closest friends. The items in the invisible second backpack are sometimes difficult for us to discuss with others. Sometimes the shame or guilt prevents us from sharing, other times it may be the pain associated with the reliving of the event. Nonetheless, we are only as sick as our secrets. This doesn't mean we should blab about our deepest and darkest degradations and humiliations. It is a suggestion that we acknowledge what we are carrying around, and recognize the impact it has on our activities of daily living, our health, and our relationships. This process can help us all heal, become more empathic to others and live more freely. Carl Jung said, "Knowing your own darkness is the best method for dealing with the darkness of other people." After all, it is difficult to enjoy the present and prepare for your future when so much of your past is weighing you down.

CHAPTER 3

JUDGING THE BOOK BY ITS COVER

When we judge a book by its cover, we may miss a great story. We all make assumptions about the lives of others. We basically judge ourselves on our intentions, and we judge others on their behavior. We seldom take the time to learn the back story. An example I often cite in my lectures has to do with a real-life example of a crisis moment in my family. My youngest daughter Dana, who has cerebral palsy and hydrocephalus, was experiencing a shunt malfunction, meaning that the tiny tube inserted in her skull was not doing its job of removing cerebral spinal fluid resulting in severe pressure on her brain. Dana was experiencing all of the classic symptoms of this malfunction including, wandering eyes, intermittent projectile vomiting, lethargy, and difficulty remaining conscious. We immediately gathered all 6 family members and jumped into our SUV and headed for the emergency department of our nearest children's hospital about 12 miles away. My driving was not of role model caliber on this afternoon. I had my hazard lights on to alert other drivers of my emergency. I was given "the middle finger" by other drivers several times as I would weave in and out of traffic. As I approached to pass slower moving traffic on the interstate, I recall some drivers throwing their hands up in exasperation with my hurry. Just as I reached my exit approximately 2 miles from the hospital, I saw police sirens in my rearview mirror. The officer approached the vehicle and asked if everything was alright. I informed him of the emergency and he quickly directed me to follow him to the entrance of the emergency room. The officer also radioed ahead as we were met by a team of emergency staff.

This is just one example of how easily and quickly individuals judge others without knowing the full story. Of course, I couldn't scream out of my SUV windows that my daughter was literally dying as the pressure from the building cerebral spinal fluid shut down her autonomic nervous system creating labored breathing and semi-consciousness. I did not have the time to construct a sign and display it as I drove at times erratically to the hospital. Most of the drivers I passed on my hasty drive were probably asking "What's wrong with that horrible driver?" I challenge you to think twice before asking, "Where did that fool learn to drive?" Instead ask, "What might have happened to cause that man to drive like a 'bat out of hell'?"

We judge others based on observable behaviors without fully knowing or understanding what drives their present actions. When we judge others, we create a distance or "judgement gap" between us that makes relationship formation unlikely. This happens in all walks of life whether in faith communities, grocery stores, corporate offices, airports, shopping malls or schools.

Many will also argue about the utility of judging for the sake of safety. In this case, there is an important difference to denote. "Making a judgement" involves deductive reasoning skills whereby "judging" in and of itself reduces an individual's entire existence to the one behavior that one had the opportunity to witness. Needless to say, we are all so much more than a snapshot of our day or a snapshot of a particular moment. I prefer to challenge my audiences when they encounter erratic, unfamiliar, bizarre, or odd behavior to "investigate, not hate." Hate will certainly prevent us from closing the "judgement gap."

CHAPTER 4

CLOSING THE JUDGMENT GAP

When we haven't taken the time to further explore our own biases through self-reflection and self-correction, the judgment gap is created.

This gap leads us to attributing characteristics to others without fully knowing the back-story. The judgment gap can be said to be the basis of numerous problems that exist in society. Relationships are the foundation of societal unity. As relationships are impeded by either individual judgments or media narratives that contribute to judgments, gaps become apparent in constructs of trust and attitude, and are perpetuated in important areas of our lives - education, health, and law. Today, there is much talk about the "achievement gap" in education, disparities in health care, and the disproportionate rates of black and brown people involved in the criminal justice arena. What if we took more time to acknowledge our own invisible second back packs and helping others to do the same, while working on unpacking all of the stuff that prevents us from being the best human beings we can possibly become? Well, people would feel more safe, less anxious and less apprehensive in our society. My invisible second backpack is not very different from the second backpacks of others. Although our traumas may be different, trauma is about the lack of safety, so the goal is restoring a sense of emotional and physical safety.

CHAPTER 5

LEARNING THE BACKSTORY

The most inherent obstacles to uncovering the issues resulting from the invisible second backpack are all of the emotions that are attached to an individual's story. Often it can be difficult to connect the story with the odd behaviors as many years can pass before the behavior begins. There is not a person alive who does not have a second backpack. As humans, we all have complications. When we avoid the humbling yet effective processes of self-reflection and self-correction, our life challenges can adversely impact the way we interact with others.

An estimated 70 percent of adults in the United States have experienced a traumatic event at least once in their lives. These events are defined as a terrifying event or ordeal that a person has experienced, witnessed, or even learned about, especially one that is life threatening or causes physical harm. The experience often causes the person to feel intense fear, horror, or a sense of helplessness. This can affect all aspects of a person's life including mental, emotional, and physical well-being. Researchers have found that prolonged trauma may disrupt and alter brain chemistry.

Here are a few examples of the invisible challenges that adults may carry around on a daily basis beyond some of the more evident issues like divorce, job stress, or chronic illnesses:

In 2015, researchers at the National Institute of Mental Health (NIMH) estimated that 16.1 million adults aged 18 or older in the United States had a least one major depressive episode in the prior year.

In, 2016, researchers at the Centers for Disease Control and Prevention (CDC) found 7.5 million women aged 15-44 with impaired fecundity (impaired ability to get pregnant or carry a baby to term).

In 2016, researchers at the National Cancer Institute (NCI) found the number of new cases of cancer (cancer incidence) to be 454.8 per 100,000 men and women per year (based on 2008-2012 cases).

In 2015, researchers at the National Alliance for Caregiving and AARP, found that approximately 43.5 million caregivers had provided unpaid care to an adult or child in the last 12 months.

In 2015, researchers at the Alzheimer's Association found that approximately 15.7 million adult family members care for someone who has Alzheimer's disease or other dementia.

The old adage, "Be kind to everyone you meet, because they are fighting battles you know nothing about," is extremely relevant today. With the emergence of social media, footage from traumatic events and scenes from traumatic encounters can be seen multiple times either voluntarily or involuntarily. I vividly recall watching the space shuttle blow up on a television screen in my elementary school classroom. Imagine viewing real-life events akin to that on a daily basis. I also can recall the events of 9-11. These events are a part of society's collective backpack, but not of my own, as I was not personally affected with someone I knew or was related to in either event.

However, children are the most vulnerable when it comes to the invisible second backpack. They can be extremely resilient and bounce back from horrific life events, however, they often lack the coping skills, coping capacity, and coping strategies to effectively deal with the weight of the issues in their second backpacks. When children have problems they are unable to talk out, they act them out. Adults do the same, but more subtly.

CHAPTER 6

SAVING THE CHILDREN

According to a survey on adverse childhood experiences by the National Survey of Children's Health (NHCS), nearly 35 million U.S. children have experienced one or more types of childhood trauma. Evidence of the significance of the implications of a child's invisible second backpack can be seen in the compilation of research assembled by the National Child Traumatic Stress Network (NCTSN):

> 60% of adults report experiencing abuse or other difficult family circumstances during childhood.
>
> 26% of children in the United States will witness or experience a traumatic event before they turn four.
>
> Four of every 10 children in America say they experienced a physical assault during the past year, with one in 10 receiving an assault-related injury.

2% of all children experienced sexual assault or sexual abuse during the past year, with the rate at nearly 11% for girls aged 14 to 17.

Nearly 14% of children repeatedly experienced maltreatment by a caregiver, including nearly 4% who experienced physical abuse.

1 in 4 children was the victim of robbery, vandalism or theft during the previous year.

More than 13% of children reported being physically bullied, while more than 1 in 3 said they had been emotionally bullied.

1 in 5 children witnessed violence in their family or the neighborhood during the previous year.

In one year, 39% of children between the ages of 12 and 17 reported witnessing violence, 17% reported being a victim of physical assault and 8% reported being the victim of sexual assault.

More than 60% of youth age 17 and younger have been exposed to crime, violence and abuse either directly or indirectly.

More than 10% of youth age 17 and younger reported five or more exposures to violence.

About 10% of children suffered from child maltreatment, were injured in an assault, or witnessed a family member assault another family member.

About 25% of youth age 17 and younger were victims of robbery or witnessed a violent act.

Nearly half of children and adolescents were assaulted at least once in the past year.

Among 536 elementary and middle school children surveyed in an inner-city community, 30% had witnessed a stabbing and 26% had witnessed a shooting.

Young children exposed to five or more significant adverse experiences in the first three years of childhood face a 76% likelihood of having one or more delays in their language, emotional or brain development.

As the number of traumatic events experienced during childhood increases, the risk of the following health problems in adulthood increases: depression; alcoholism; drug abuse; suicide attempts; heart and liver diseases; pregnancy problems; high stress; uncontrollable anger; and family, financial, and job related problems.

These data represent what is in the invisible second backpack that is driving the behavior that we see in our families, schools, and communities. It is important to note that not all children will experience trauma in the same way. And not all behavioral and emotional problems are related to trauma. In fact, although research and statistics provide "predictable and controlled" study group data, every person is a unique study of one.

Studies do show that children who are hurt either emotionally or physically are more likely to become defiant, angry, aggressive, sad, anxious or withdrawn. Since the goal of every caring adult in a child's life should be to ensure that the child is challenged, healthy, engaged, safe, and supported, when abuse occurs, a child's feelings of safety and protection have been violated. These feelings can continue to build inside of children through adulthood.

The invisible second backpack contains the backstory. If ever there is something that doesn't quite make sense or meet the eye, investigate the second backpack. We can better understand unsafe behavior as an expression of how unsafe this individual feels.

I have been fortunate to be a part of teams with data-driven and empirically based programs in prevention, trauma-healing and resiliency training programs for children who have experienced trauma. The programs have been effectively used with adults and children in the educational, juvenile justice, mental health, corporate, and medical systems. When we do not have programs that adequately address these issues, we tend to further traumatize already traumatized children and adults.

As an educator and clinical psychologist, I have seen firsthand how difficult some young people can be. However, I optimistically believe, as does Plato, that every child is equipped with extraordinary potential to be successful, and the purpose of education is to help expose that potential. The next chapter will provide a summary of programs that have proven hopeful and helpful for changing the future of children who are weighed down by their invisible second backpacks. Adult programs are systematically addressed through personal and professional development lectures, seminars and workshops.

CHAPTER 7

TEACHING ALL STUDENTS

By effectively teaching all students, we change the odds of the detrimental effects of the excess baggage that children carry with them daily. Of foremost importance to educators is not necessarily changing the conditions in which children live, but understanding the lives children live.

Heavy baggage can erode a student's sense of hope and optimism. I am convinced that quality schools with high performing educators who teach all students, are among the greatest opportunity equalizers for disparities in society as well as promoters of student success.

With this in mind, the following steps should be undertaken:

> **First,** we should adhere to the Latin phrase "primum non nocere" that means **"first do no harm."**
> **Second**, everyone must know his or her role. As a high performing educator, one must provide clear,

relevant, and attainable goals and be available to offer assistance as needed. The foundation of a secure relationship is built by meeting needs. It is the parent's or guardian's responsibility to get the child to school, the child's responsibility to do the assigned work, the educator's responsibility to ensure the work is worth doing, and the principal's responsibility to make sure the school is worth attending.

Third, educators must take great care not to indulge in the common assumptions concerning students who are challenging to teach. I often remind educators that *we must teach the students we have and not the ones we wish we had.*

Fourth, it is important to know that every student is a study of one. There is no particular all-encompassing profile for a student laden with a heavy second backpack. Traumatized students come in all shapes and sizes. The attackers get most of our attention because they are often seen and heard, but the avoiders can be just as traumatized if not more, however they often go invisible.

Fifth, promote a sense of internal control and self-efficacy. Psychologist Albert Bandura has defined self-efficacy as one's belief in one's ability to succeed in specific situations or accomplish a task. This reflects confidence in one's ability to exert control over one's own motivation, behavior and social environment.

Sixth, have high yet realistic expectations. Having a second backpack does not constitute having a disability, and disability does not mean inability. In my opinion, a *disability in education should be about not seeing ability* in all students. High performing educators help students use their backpacks as jetpacks by teaching students about resiliency. We become what we overcome.

Seventh, recognize that the tenets of good teaching are quite similar to those of good parenting. Be firm, fun and fair. Lastly, although their behavior may seem as if they do not want support and encouragement, don't give up on them. We all want support and encouragement.

CHAPTER 8

UNPACKING EMOTIONAL BAGGAGE

These are only a few programs, or as I prefer to say "philosophies" that are designed to respond to adverse childhood experiences by building resilience, identifying and healing trauma early, and improving a child's social and emotional development. It is also important to familiarize yourself with the types of events that people, especially children, find traumatic as well as the various accompanying symptoms.

The following approaches have been found to be highly successful strategies for not abandoning the young people who need our help the most. Restorative justice policy is a more productive alternative to zero-tolerance policies. Restorative justice both allows for and encourages improvement for the highest risk youth. A central tenet to help alleviate the stress and trauma associated with the second backpack should be to include professional, or formally trained, monitored and evaluated mentors. Professional mentoring works. When a student's second backpack leads them to engage in behavior that would result in emotional or physical harm, school suspension, expulsions or arrest, we can (and should) offer them professional mentoring.

The Invisible Second Backpack -Trauma–informed or trauma-sensitive teaching (Dr. Adolph Brown, et al., The Leadership & Learning Institute):

> This is an on-going series of trainings designed to provide teachers and other staff with the science and skills to better manage traumatized students in the classroom. The focus of the training is to ask teachers and staff to examine their tone, attitudes, perceptions and biases when communicating with all children, but especially children with histories of trauma.

The Professional School Based Mentoring (PSBM) Program (Dr. Adolph Brown & Mr. Joseph Beaman, The Leadership & Learning Institute):

> This program is a "Best Practice" whereby teachers are trained to become Professional School Based Mentors (PSBM) as a resource to build capacity, effectively engage family & community, and achieve

positive student outcomes. The program developers recognize that our highest risk students DO NOT constitute a homogeneous cluster of children with like characteristics. The program developers skillfully and willfully address the gifted learner with anxiety issues as well as the angry learner with family problems. The PSBM helps the youth understand the harm in their behavior, why it is a poor choice, and how to fix it. Attention is given to how our students struggle outside of the classroom from the effects of severely dysfunctional families, gang violence, poverty and hunger. This philosophy has also been used in conjunction with restorative justice measures whereby suspended students would be referred to day(s) in the mentorship program on school property.

Positive Behavior Supports (PBS) & Culturally Responsive Positive Behavior Interventions and Supports (CR-PBIS) (Drs. Adolph Brown, III & William Combs, The Leadership & Learning Institute):

This philosophy teaches educators to adequately address the needs of high-risk behavior students by identifying misbehavior, modeling appropriate behaviors, and providing clear consequences for behavior in the classroom context. The culturally responsive component embodies a method of teaching and learning that builds on and values the cultural experiences and knowledge of all participants.

Restorative Justice Framework (Ron Claassen, Director of Restorative Justice in Schools):

> This framework is based on respect, responsibility, relationship-building and relationship-repairing. It focuses on mediation and agreement rather than punishment. The goals of the program are to keep children in school and to create a safe environment where learning can flourish. When a student misbehaves, he or she is given the opportunity to come forward and make things right. He or she sits down in a circle and works together with the teacher and the affected parties to work it out.

These programs are all effective in improving school culture and providing a new approach to school discipline.

CHAPTER 9

COMING TOGETHER FOR CHILDREN WHO ARE FALLING APART

In Kijita (Wajita), there is a proverb which says "Omwana ni wa bhone," meaning "regardless of a child's biological parent(s) its upbringing belongs to the community." This perspective is not only about community, it emphasizes collaboration. This view challenges Western individualism. As a child living in the inner-city projects, and even as a child visiting my grandfather in the rural areas of Virginia, my conduct was of concern to everyone, not just my mother, especially if it involved behaving badly. Any adult had the authority to discipline or rebuke me and would make my misdeeds known to my mother who in turn would also punish me further. This was an attempt to preserve the moral well-being of the community. If we do not have a community-minded approach with all children, especially those with tremendous loads in their backpack, we will continue to feed the disparaging pipelines of "school to street" (suspension) and "school to prison." Our future is at stake, yet many in society and schools fail to work concertedly for our children.

In, Rwanda there is a saying, that "The dancers have changed, but the drums are the same." I have sadly witnessed this on numerous occasions when a family is reluctant to receive assistance for a troubled child or challenging family matter. The reasons are vast and can certainly point to the content of second backpacks of the individual family members. Often, families experience of shame, guilt or humiliation prevent them for getting help. If we "intentionally engage" families, meaning, understanding that each family is a "study of one" and allowing opportunity for each to be heard, respected and valued, we start solving this crisis and closing toxic pipelines.

To engage with anyone, per the first chapter of this book, you first need to know their story. The basics of knowing someone's story remains the same – before starting to discover other people's stories we must first have a clear perspective of our own story. At this point we are capable of demonstrating transparency, honesty and a willingness to listen and improve.

This is much deeper than doing something purely for the sake of checking a box on a report; an activity I have found that many of my education and corporate colleagues alike frequently participate.

Many education and corporate leaders are also reluctant to receive "outside help" from consultants, speakers, trainers and best practices philosophies for fear of looking like an inadequate leader. The opposite is true here. Not staying abreast of best practices and being fearful of shared success makes one look less than capable of leading. The bottom line is, whatever can effectively and efficiently help the situation should be welcomed and sustained over time. The grave reality in both education and corporations is that fact that it often boils down to priorities and politics. Politics should never circumvent the needs of our young.

CHAPTER 10

SPREADING LOVE, LIGHT, & INSIGHT

I have committed myself to a professional journey of spreading love, light and insight. I translate this mission as one of healing, transformation and education. These are the very tools that have helped countless individuals live their best lives regardless of language, age, race, religion, education, social status, gender, and sexual orientation.

It is my hope that this book serves as a valuable resource and reminder for adults and children, and ultimately heals the child within the adult.

The invisible backpack provides *insight* into some of the possible reasons that people behave the way they do. Once we understand someone's behavior, we can chose to accept it or attempt to help them correct it. I live by the saying, "I didn't come to teach you, I came to *love* you, and love will teach you." The *light* becomes more evident as we develop the courage to uncover or unpack our deepest and darkest hurts and pains.

Ultimately, if we spread love, light and insight to the individuals who are the most challenging to love, have very little sunshine in their darkest moments, and behavior challenges that lead them astray, we can collectively understand the meaning behind their behavior, learn to take things seriously not personally, and become a beacon of light for them on their journey.

"Do not train a child to learn by force or harshness; but direct them to it by what amuses their minds, so that you may be better able to discover with accuracy the peculiar bent of the genius of each."

—*Plato*

Please consider using the following pages of this book to unpack your own backpacks. Self-reflection is a humbling process. It's essential to find out why you think, say and do certain things...then better yourself. Self-reflection and self-correction are the highest forms of self-learning and healing.

Based on reading this book, what are the most important professional and personal issues you have identified? How will you address these issues?

_____

_____

_____

_____

_____

_____

_____

_____

Based on reading this book, what are the most important professional and personal issues you have identified? How will you address these issues?

_____

_____

_____

_____

_____

_____

_____

_____

Based on reading this book, what are the most important professional and personal issues you have identified? How will you address these issues?

_____

_____

_____

_____

_____

_____

_____

_____

_____

Based on reading this book, what are the most important professional and personal issues you have identified? How will you address these issues?

_____

_____

_____

_____

_____

_____

_____

_____

_____

_____

Based on reading this book, what are the most important professional and personal issues you have identified? How will you address these issues?

_____

_____

_____

_____

_____

_____

_____

_____

_____

Based on reading this book, what are the most important professional and personal issues you have identified? How will you address these issues?

_____

_____

_____

_____

_____

_____

_____

_____

_____

_____

CPSIA information can be obtained
at www.ICGtesting.com
Printed in the USA
LVHW022353220721
693426LV00012B/1101